To Be In CHRIST

To Be In
CHRIST

Hubert van Zeller

with an appreciation by
David Steindl-Rast

Crossroad · New York

1981
The Crossroad Publishing Company
575 Lexington Avenue, New York, NY 10022

Printed in the United States of America

Book design: Catherine Gallagher

Library of Congress Cataloging in Publication Data

Van Zeller, Hubert, 1905-
To be in Christ.

1. Meditations. I. Title.
BX2182.2.V32 1981 242 81-9793
ISBN 0-8245-0086-5 AACR2

CONTENTS

PREFACE

In an age of departmentalism and specialization we tend to divide rather than to unify. This is seen in the religious way of thinking as much as in any other. While allowing the necessity of putting certain subjects under headings there is nevertheless the need to see the principle which governs what is put under headings. The gospels and epistles teach many things, the catechism teaches many things, the church comes out with pin-pointing encyclicals, the liturgy is far from uniform. This is right and clearly what God wills. But God also wants simplicity in outlook and service. It is the present writer's purpose to indicate the unifying elements in our acceptance of religion, stressing the harmony of different graces working under the same Spirit. The love which animated our Lord—which *is* our Lord—animated also our Lady and the saints. Not three kinds of love but one. Everything about religion, about theology, about Scripture, about sacraments, is a facet of love.

TO LIVE IN CHRIST

To live in Christ is, in the widest sense, to live in a state of grace. It is a gift but a gift which God does not deny to anyone. What we are more particularly considering in these pages is the development of the gift. All are invited to develop the life of Christ in the soul, and those who set themselves to do so are actively and progressively on the way to identification: identification with the divine person so far as is possible in this life, leading to the fullest identification to be enjoyed eternally in heaven. Christ incorporates us into his life at baptism, offers his life to us in countless ways as we mature in our religious formation, and finally crowns us with the grace of divine union.

Though baptism and religious service create the disposition, they do not constitute the unitive habit as understood by the classical mystical writers. Union for them means assimilation. It is not our good works that can force an entry into Christ's life. It is God's grace, prepared for by good works and prayer, that enables us to rise above and beyond ourselves and to be assumed into the fully meritorious life of Christ. His merits are our claim: we have no claim of our own. A rough analogy would be the way in which vapor is contained in the cloud. We are not only supported by Christ's life in us, as moisture is supported in a cloud, but we can so increase this dependence as ultimately to be absorbed into it. Vapor becomes cloud and cloud is vapor. "I live now not I but Christ lives in me." I am nothing but what I am in Christ. This is true integration and the realization of our purpose as souls created in likeness of God. This is human life in its fullness, waiting for participation in the divine life which is heaven.

So how are we to set about it? While the process is to be seen primarily as the way in which God sets about it, there are practical steps which can be directed by us. Confession, Communion, the Mass. Frequent confession is played down today but if we are trying to enter into the sinless life of Jesus, the more often we cleanse ourselves of sin and guilt the better. Those who go to confession rarely, and some have dropped the use of this sacrament altogether, are in danger of blunting the sensibility to sin and are accordingly approaching the deepest reality of religion, and consequently of the interior life, in a spirit of presumption. "Where there is to be union of two," says St. Bernard, "there must be correspondence of extremities." Though we may not perfectly comprehend we can at least correspond, and the measures available are particularly the sacraments of penance and Holy Communion, and a deeper appreciation of the Mass.

Whilst baptism is the most necessary of the sacraments—not only because it removes the stain of original sin and incorporates the soul into the mystical body of Christ, but also because without it the other sacraments cannot be received—the sacrament of the holy Eucharist is designated by St. Thomas as the "most excellent." So the most immediate and effective way of living in Christ is by receiving the bread of life. "By the mystery of this water and wine," the priest prays in the Mass, "let us come to share in the divinity of Christ who humbled himself to share in our humanity." The elements of the Eucharist are the outward signs of the inward grace which is union with the life of Christ. □

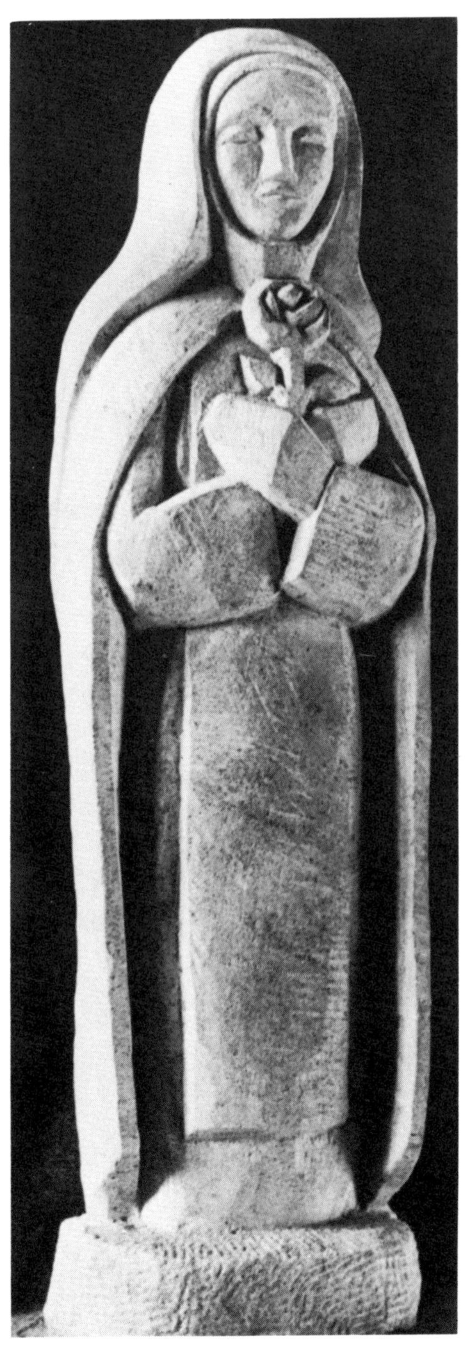

TO LOVE IN CHRIST

It follows logically from the foregoing that if we live Christ's life we love with Christ's love. His life is all love; his spirit is all love. It is not so much that his love "rubs off" on us but that it actually animates us and "informs" our every activity. We breathe his spirit, and since his spirit is love we love with his love. Our love such as it is, is nothing without grace, nothing without his spirit. We have not invented what love there is in us; we cannot fashion charity as we can fashion a rose garden or an omelette. The most we can do is direct it from him within us to him outside us. Our love for others, provided it is in charity and not in worldly desire, is the response of divine love to the attraction of divine love. We may not be aware of the supernatural quality of the process, but this is what is happening: like stretching out to like: the magnetic attraction of part to part—in this case, part to *whole*—making one.

"The way we know that we remain in him and he in us," says St. John in his epistle, "is that he has given us of his spirit." His spirit is his gift, as his life is his gift. The consequence is stated simply by St. John: "If he has so loved us, we must have the same love for one another."

If God is the source and principle of charity towards others, it should not be difficult for us to judge between what is loving in Christ and what is loving in worldly love. Am I expressing him who dwells within me or am I exploiting an emotion to gratify myself? Since Jesus expressed his love towards the Father and towards man in terms of sacrifice, we, if we are in union with him, must express our love in the same way. Again the test is easy to apply: am I ready to go any lengths in sacrificing myself for God's sake and for the sake of other people? "Greater love than this no man has than that he would lay down his life for his fellow men." True love, whether towards God or man, transcends self, leaves personal satisfaction aside. This willingness to forgo the selfish element in fact brings about its own reward: we love in peace and without guilt. Our love is no less strong because we have detached it from passion; it is all the more strong because we are drawing our love from the fount of love itself.

Since in the creation of man God designed love to be of one piece, the divisions of love caused by sin and selfishness must inevitably lead to the confusions we experience in our affections: jealousy, romantic fantasy, doubt, lack of clear judgment, loneliness, resentment and dramatization.

In the days when ink was used in the classroom, boys were in the habit of folding a piece of paper, dropping some ink into the line of the fold, pressing the two halves together, and then opening the paper to see how the two patterns corresponded. Ideally the patterns should match one another exactly. So should the two articulations, coming from the one foundation, of charity. But they rarely do. One side may be clear while the other is blotted and blotched. Where in a soul of prayer there is no room for compassion, the assumption is that one side has been pressed too hard and the other not hard enough. "All of you are one in Jesus Christ," says St. Paul. "Let us become gods for him," comments St. Gregory of Nyssa, "since he became man for us." □

TO PRAY IN CHRIST

When the Church concludes its official prayers with the words "Through Christ our Lord," it is not just repeating a formula or letting the faithful know that the prayer has come to an end. The Church means it—theologically. Whether we state it explicitly or not, all our prayers are made through Christ and in him and with him. If they are not, they are abstract prayers, and not Christian prayers at all. Christian prayer assumes the communication between the Son and the Father, and, implicitly at least, moves into the relationship. Christian prayer does not tie itself down to the consideration of episodes in our Lord's life and to the mysteries of the gospel. Christian prayer may even, in the act of contemplation for instance, discourage the use of meditative forms which recall scenes and promote speculation. But for a Christian to imagine that there could be communication between the soul and the Father apart from the meditation of the Son would be unorthodox: would be to miss the significance of the incarnation. "No man comes to the Father," said our Lord, "but through me . . . I am in the Father and the Father is in me."

In praying to the Father Jesus had no need to pray through anyone's intercession or on the strength of anyone's prayer. Since he was God he was at all times united with the Father and acting in perfect harmony with the Spirit. His prayer emerged accordingly. He needed no impulse of grace in order to pray: he *was* grace. We on the other hand need grace at every moment of our lives, and our prayer depends on it. "Without me you can do nothing." Without him we cannot even begin to pray. His prayer is our attraction to prayer, and its substance when once we have begun. We have no inspiration of our own. "No one can say 'Jesus is the Lord,' " St. Paul reminds the Corinthians, "except in the Holy Spirit."

What of the prayers of non-Christians, and of the souls of the Old Testament? Though non-Christians certainly pray, and seem to have done so since the earliest ages of man, they nevertheless need the grace of the Spirit. In the same way the prayers and sacrifices of the Old Law glorified God at the inspiration and by the power of the Spirit. It can be said that in unconscious anticipation of, and in virtue of, Christ's prayer and sacrifice, the worship offered by the Hebrew people was made pleasing to the Father. When Jesus came and prayed, he took up the prayer of all mankind and of every generation, and gave it a place in his own.

Thus the stuttering, distracted, inadequate praises of groping humanity become, in the alchemy of grace, divine.

In an airport a small boy is playing with a toy airplane. He makes the appropriate sounds: the shrill squeal, the roar of the engine, the bumping along the runway, the even humming after the take-off. After actual boarding, the noises of the jet which he has been imitating take over, catching up the child's voice into the authentic vibrations. The analogy is far from exact because prayer, however elementary, is never a matter of make-believe; it is nevertheless an imperfect and amateurish rendering of the real thing. The real thing is what carries us into the sky.

So in prayer our operation is secondary; the primary operation is God's—and our cooperation with it. □

TO THINK IN CHRIST

St. Paul exhorts us to "have the mind of Christ." He knows that if we think as Jesus thinks we shall be living in charity, and he will be living in us. It must follow that our works, values, decisions and prayers will carry the seal of his spirit. "There are three things which characterize a Christian," says St. Gregory of Nyssa in his *Christian Perfection,* "namely action, speech, thought. The origin of every word is thought. After thinking comes speech, which reveals in words the idea which has been conceived in the mind. After thought and speech comes action, which realizes the thoughts in deeds." Later in the same treatise St. Gregory elaborates as follows:

"That which is pure of every inclination to passion tends toward the source of tranquility, Christ. If a man draws from Christ his thoughts he will reveal in himself a likeness to his pattern . . . purity has only one nature, both that which is in Christ and that which is in the one who shares in him: the one who shares in him draws from him and brings beauty of thought to his life . . . so there is a harmony when uprightness of life is joined with thoughts which are inspired by Christ."

The ability to think in Christ is not just a knack of the mind, a habit acquired by the belief that it is the most sensible way to go about things: it is a gift, a grace. Even in the human relationship between friends it would be impossible for both to think alike—on any subject, let alone on all subjects—unless the one had imparted his thought to the other. Jesus gives us his thinking provided we pray for it and are serious in trying to shape our lives according to his teaching. It is as a consequence of our prayer life that we hold up to his judgment the circumstances which face us, and it is on the findings of this submission that we come to judge as he judges, to think as he thinks.

Not only are we confronted every day with situations involving personal behavior, but we are expected to have an opinion on the larger issues as well. Obviously, when called upon to give advice to an individual as to how he should act in a spiritual or moral contingency, we should ask for the light to handle the question as Jesus would handle it. Less obviously we should pray for light when challenged by the prevailing thought on secular matters. How do we view social, political, economic, nationalistic questions? Are our minds conditioned by the press or by the gospel? Do we defer to this or that leader's practical judgment, or do we direct the doubt to Jesus for enlightenment? What does Jesus at this moment think of equal rights for women, of hunger strikes, of capital punishment, of the right to refuse "extraordinary" means to prolong life? Have I ever referred these things in prayer to him? If not I can hardly claim to be fostering his thought in me and to be sharing his mind.

"In your light," proclaims the psalmist, "we shall see light," and only in his light. He is the light of the world, and if this light burns within us, we are lamps which shine to others in a darkened world. We are not our own light; we are light reflected from him whose light and life we share. As such we bring the thought of Jesus to those who think wrongly or who do not think at all. □

TO SPEAK IN CHRIST

In taking on man's human nature, Jesus took on man's human powers and skills. Among the powers was the power of speech, and every word he uttered was to the glory of the Father. Among the skills was the ability to make tables and chairs, and everything he turned out was again to the glory of God. We are here more concerned with the gift of speech than with the gift of being able to handle a carpenter's tools perfectly.

The gift of communication by word of mouth is granted in the natural order to all except the dumb, and as in the case of all other gifts, the question depends upon how it is used. St. James asks how the one spring can "gush forth fresh water and foul," how a fig tree can "produce olives or a grapevine figs" . . . yet "blessing and cursing come out of the same mouth." "I assure you," our

Lord himself says, "on judgment day people will be held accountable for every unguarded word they speak. By your words you will be acquitted and by your words you will be condemned." It is estimated that the average person speaks roughly 18,000 words a day. (I would have thought it might be more.) How are we to cut down on unguarded and "idle" words? How are we to see that only clear water comes from the spring and that fruit trees produce only their appropriate fruit? Resolutions help of course—deciding to be more charitable in what we say, avoiding gossip, telling the truth, suppressing salacious talk and bad language—but a surer way is to let the spirit of Jesus penetrate our spirit and transform it so that it becomes his.

In the light of the parable of the two sons, one of whom said he would work in his father's field and stayed where he was, while the other said he would not go yet eventually went, it is curious that Jesus should make words the deciding factor between acquittal and condemnation. There is no real contradiction, however, and what he surely meant us to understand was that while the main consideration must be the attitude of the mind and heart—the interior choosing—the exterior of expression is found in speech. Just as an air bubble under water forces itself to the surface, so what is good or evil below the surface in our character comes out in the form of what we say.

If this is so, then people who are habitually united with Jesus within will reflect him in their conversation. This does not mean that pieties will flow from their lips. There is all the difference between sanctity and sanctimoniousness. It means that what they say, coming as it does from a different level within themselves, will reach souls at a different level. Jesus in one soul will move out to Jesus in another. There will be a corresponding exchange. The man who is reliving the life of Jesus has no desire to edify, but those who talk to him come away the better for it.

Then there is the question of preaching and directing. Here again the words are the echo of the Word. If the man in the pulpit and the confessional is the man he is supposed to be, namely the man of prayer, then what he says will be what Jesus wants him to say—what Jesus himself is saying through the man's mouth. If a sermon is worth anything it must come from God, and, through the souls addressed, be directed back to God. "The words that go forth from my lips, says the Lord, must not return to me void." This is from Isaias, who knew well that he was only God's mouthpiece. □

TO ACT IN CHRIST

"Man sees the appearance" the Lord told Samuel, "but the Lord looks into the heart." When we speak today of the heart we think of the emotions, and because we know that religion and spirituality are to do primarily with the will, we tend to be suspicious of references to the heart in the literature of the spirit. But since the Bible mentions the word 176 times, we can conclude that the heart is above reproach. As the *terminus a quo* the heart should be thought of as the most significant area in the human makeup. What comes from the heart gives to human action its character. The heart is more, even, than the launching pad: it accompanies the rocket on its flight.

If there is nothing in the heart, there will be nothing to show. *Ex nihilo nihil fit.* If the heart is possessed by Christ, there will be everything to show. Another scholastic axiom is *actio sequitur esse,* which means that what we are will declare itself in what we do. If we have no thought of the supernatural, we achieve only natural results. "In order to paint the mysteries of Christ," Fra Angelica is believed to have said, "you must make your home in the mysteries of Christ." The same idea is echoed by Jacob Epstein: "You can copy Greek sculpture and get the look of it, but if you are to get the feel of Greek sculpture you must think as the Greeks did."

Having instanced the parable of the two sons, we can cite here another two sons, Cain and Abel. What mattered to God more than the offerings themselves was the attitude which prompted the offerings. The objects sacrificed were the outward evidence, the symbol almost, when it was the inward dispositions that qualified. The same may be seen in the parable of the Pharisee and the publican. In our present context the conclusion to be drawn is that unless I live Christ's life, totally accepting his values, I live the world's life and will find myself being conditioned by its values.

In proposing to himself to work for God and not for worldly considerations, the serious Christian has to create for himself an environment which does not admit of compromise. He is not now concerned so much with good and evil but with good and better. The pull of grace is for him the pull towards evangelical perfection. It is not even as if he were embarking upon a career; it is more a question of allowing a certain way of life—a way of life resulting from a response to grace—to mold him. He accepts what God has chosen for him, and what God has chosen for him is his own divine life. It is not something which souls have to learn out of a book or arrive at by practicing certain rituals, devotional and ascetical.

"I do not think that people are good because they have read instructions to be good. I believe that they become good because their souls have been penetrated with the goodness of God, because the Holy Spirit is in them with the Love of the Father and the example and redemptive sacrifice of the Son."

And again: "The energy of a man depends on the life of the idea within him." * It is the underlying idea, pervaded by grace, which alone gives to man's action its merit. □

* William Rees-Mogg, *An Humble Heaven* (Hamish Hamilton) pp 26 and 55.

THE ACCEPTANCE OF JESUS

That Jesus accepted the Father's will at every moment of his life is not in question. That he submitted to the yoke of the Roman occupation and to the authority of the levitical priesthood is clear from a number of incidents recorded in the gospels. What we are more concerned with here is with such everyday circumstances as we might ourselves experience. His patience must often have been tried by the obtuseness of his disciples, by the tepid service given to the Father on the part of those who considered themselves religious, by the disappointments he met with in his work, by the legalism and exaggerated ritualism which prevailed everywhere he turned, by the want of consistency and above all by the absence of love.

What our Lord was unable to correct he put up with. In this he was not compromising or condoning: he was reconciling the immediate with the eternal, he was referring the actual outcome of God's gifts to man to God himself whose will it was that man should use the gifts freely. Jesus could have overthrown the Roman Empire and levelled the Jewish Temple to the ground. Instead he surrendered and left everything in God's hands. The Father must be allowed to do things in his own way and in his own time. Failing to learn from Christ's example, we resist the dispositions of divine providence, and feel frustrated, discouraged, disillusioned. We would do better to bow to the limitations of the inevitable, and to work constructively on the existing material. The ideal is not the realization of what we have planned but the supernaturalizing of what lies to hand.

There is a Greek legend which tells of a people living on an island who were warned by one of the gods that a great wave would soon sweep over them bringing total destruction. The islanders, assembling together to discuss how the impending disaster might be met, sought the advice of the island's elders. The first wise man to get up suggested that a temple to the gods should be built and though it would not be finished in time, the undertaking would at least show that divine favor was invoked, which would ensure a propitious standing in the after life. The second elder to be consulted gave his opinion that if all the inhabitants, forgetting their differences, were to open their doors in hospitality the gods would reward them by keeping them together in the next world and thus sparing them from the loneliness of death. The third wise man was very old, and when the matter was at some length made clear to him, he said, "We must learn to live under water."

The terms of human existence are given us by God. We are born into a fallen world; we grow up with grand ideas of bettering this fallen world; we find in later life that our hopes have come to nothing, that our efforts have been wasted, that there is not a thing we can do about it. Either we make the act of faith or sulk. Our Lord could have avoided disappointment but he went ahead and accepted it. He could have avoided temptation but endured it. St. Paul, after experiencing disappointment and temptation, was able to say, "In whatever state I am I am content therewith.' Contentment—so much easier to gauge than happiness—comes of surrender and not of achievement, not in the fulfilling of desires but in seeing God's hand in the dealing of the cards. □

THE FIRMNESS OF JESUS

Following what has been said about Jesus accepting his place in the pattern of life willed for him by the Father, we should not forget how forthright he was in laying down the principles which it was his mission to teach. Where truth, love, morality, the Father's glory were concerned, he did not yield an inch to the prevailing pressures. In fact he went beyond the accepted moral standards of the Law. "You have heard that it was said to them of old 'Thou shalt not kill,' but I say to you whosoever is angry with his brother . . . you have heard that it was said to them of old 'Thou shalt not commit adultery,' but I say to you whosoever shall look on a woman to lust after her . . . " This "I say to you" was repeated when bringing up the question of swearing by sacred things, of lending and retaliation, of loving enemies and of practicing generosity. Moreover, what he told his hearers about the right way to pray and the right way to fast must have seemed a new way indeed of looking at these things. Jesus was teaching as *one having power* and not as the scribes and Pharisees. "You cannot serve God and mammon." There was no compromise here.

Nor could his audiences have seen in Jesus' preaching either the humanist reformer's high moral purpose or the blazing idealism of the fanatic. Whether they believed in his divinity or not, whether they believed he had been sent by God or not, they recognized his authoritative religious voice. As they listened to him over the years of his public ministry they were witnesses of his intransigence. In fact it was his obstinate tenacity which earned him his condemnation and crucifixion. Contemporary culture, Jewish and Roman alike, observed a much more flexible code than that which Jesus proclaimed.

Influenced by the hymnal image of Jesus "meek and mild," we adjust awkwardly to the Jesus who could be violent enough to fling the money changers out of the temple. We almost make excuses for his anger, citing the theological term "propassion," but whether he was fighting abuses or the Pharisees, he was showing a side of his nature which is shared by all of us, and without apology. One wonders if he was not nearer to the Boanerges, the sons of thunder, than is generally supposed. In charging his disciples with lack of faith he could equally have charged them with lack of spirit, and it was only after they had received his Holy Spirit at Pentecost that they took a strong line. St. Peter's experience in Pilate's court shows us the need for moral courage—an aspect of moral courage which trust in God's grace can alone guarantee.

Most of us practicing Christians are firm enough in our convictions but are we firm enough in bearing witness to our convictions? We have not only to keep the faith but to give an account of it and defend it. The faith is not something which it can be left to the catechists to put across in instructions to children and prospective converts. It is something which we promulgate by the firmness of our commitment. It requires both moral courage and perseverance to build a city seated upon a hill. If we are to be the salt of the earth and the light of the world, we may not hide behind an appellative Christianity and hope for the best. Truth demands the evidence of those who hold the truth. If our Lord did not water down what he had said in the Sermon on the Mount, his followers may not either. □

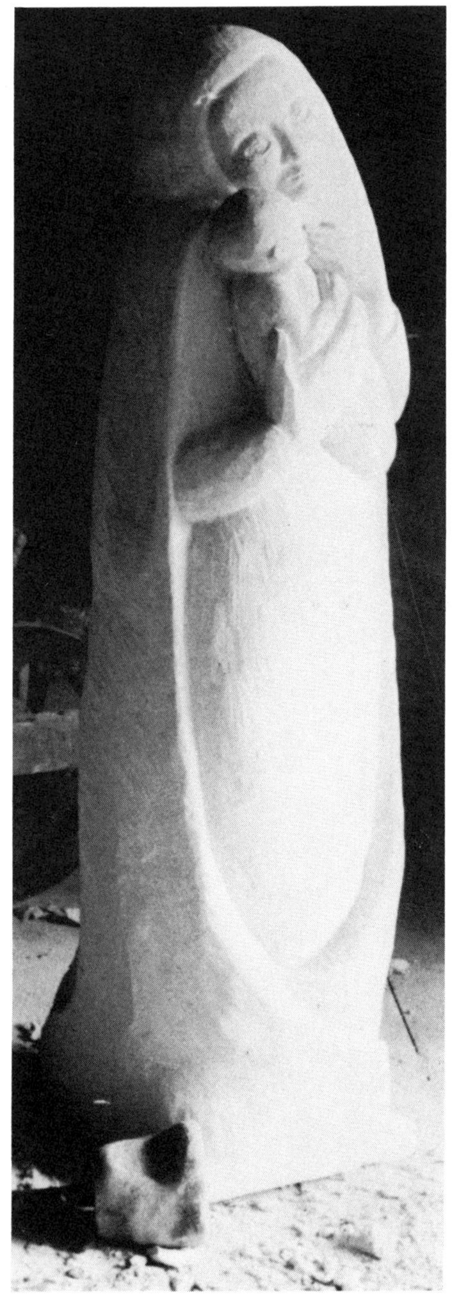

THE ACCESSIBILITY OF JESUS

In spite of the uncompromising nature of his doctrine, there was nothing of the harshness about Jesus which is sometimes found in religious people. He could be stern as we have seen, but he was never dismissive. Love itself, love from whom all humanity springs, how could he have been unlovable? The word "amiable" (admittedly a weak word to act as an adjective to Jesus, and one which describes only a manner), derives from the Latin "amabilis." Critical commentators have made much of the absence of any reference in the gospels to our Lord laughing or smiling. The implication is that his facial expression was forbidding rather than welcoming. How, we ask, can an unsmiling man be reconciled with the concept of the perfectly rounded human being? This is an invalid application of the argument from silence. It should be pointed out by way of answer that nowhere in the gospel is Jesus recorded as yawning, swinging his arms, wiping his forehead or any of the hundred actions we perform every day and which are as instinctive as smiling. Had he never smiled, our Lord would never have drawn children to himself, and surely the act of bringing Zacchaeus down from the branches of the sycamore tree was accompanied by friendly laughter. And were those sermons preached without hint of a lighter side? And were those parables—especially the ones which needed changes of voice—delivered lrimly and without a spark of humor? Also if Jesus had been even slightly unapproachable in the face he showed to the world he would not have been so thronged by people as not to have time to eat. I doubt if people today would ask a well-known figure who glared at them to sign their autograph books.

Whereas modern theater has gone to one extreme about Jesus, interpreting his humanity as hilarity, the film world has gone to the other extreme, making him sombre, dreamy and without spirit. To rob him of his dignity is to rob him of his divinity as well; to rob him of his joy is to rob him of his union with the Father. There are enough barriers to our communication with him as it is, without presenting him as either an entertainer or a visionary, remote and aloof. How can we give our confidence to someone who is either clowning or else wafting in ecstasy in a world beyond our reach?

So what conclusions can we draw in relating all this to our Christian service? Since Christ dwells within us and is the principle of our activity, our contacts with other people must take their character from his. Like him and with him we must be at the disposal of others, never so withdrawn into recollection as to be dismissive. The prayer life must be safeguarded certainly, or we shall have nothing at the supernatural level to give out, but our contemplation may not serve as an excuse for cutting ourselves off from our fellow members in the mystical body of Christ. The mystical life and the mystical body go together. The mystical Jesus is at the same time the accessible Jesus, and we share his spirit. □

THE UNIVERSALITY OF JESUS

Our Lord makes it clear in his last discourse to his disciples that his prayer, and therefore his work of salvation, is not for them only but for all. He prays to the Father "that the world may believe that you sent me . . . so shall the world know that you sent me." If our Christianity truly reflects the mind of Christ animating our minds, it must look to the whole of mankind. If it is to be a supernatural religion and not a sectarian movement, it must be supranational: no racial, cultural, political divisions. Jesus prayed that his followers might be one—"that *all* may be one, as you, Father, are in me and I in you"—and though his followers have never yet been so united, the ideal of unity and catholicity still holds and must always hold. A nationalistic religion may serve a cause but does not serve God. The more religion is identified with an ethnic body, the farther it is removed from the body of Christ. "Go ye into the whole world and preach the gospel to every creature, to all nations." Even more absurd than the idea of a Christianity for a particular caste or color would be a Christianity for one level of society and not another, for one economic grouping and not another.

It is true that the kingdom of God was first preached to "the lost sheep of the house of Israel." Jesus gave to those who had been the chosen people the chance, before all others, of belonging to the universal Church; but the "good news" was for all mankind. This is brought out in a number of parables, especially those of the vineyard left untended and given to others, the supper to which guests of every sort were admitted, the mustard tree, the net cast into the sea. Nor were the miracles for the Jews alone: witness the Syrophoenician woman whose daughter was cured and the Roman centurion who begged a cure for his servant. A further indication that the gospel message was for all mankind might be seen in our Lord's words: "If *any* man thirsts let him come to me and drink," and "*whosoever* does not carry his cross and come after me can not become my disciple."

So the Judaism of Jesus was no restriction. There is nothing in the Sermon on the Mount which would not equally apply to a Buddhist or a Hindu; indeed much of it is parallelled in Chinese and Hindu literature. It is true that Jewish converts did not at once take to the notion of a universal church, and even St. Peter had to be shown in a vision that gentiles were to be encouraged to join, but St. Paul, happy to call himself "teacher of the nations," stressed repeatedly the doctrine of grace and salvation to all. The opportunity is open to everybody, even if not everybody takes advantage of it. (To the Corinthians: "It was in one Spirit that all of us, whether Jew or Greek, slave or free, were baptized into one body." To the Romans: "Does God belong to the Jews alone? Is he not also the God of the gentiles?" To the Galatians: "There does not exist among you Jew or Greek, slave or freeman, male or female; all are one in Christ Jesus.") In the City of God, everyone is a first class citizen; in the Body of Christ, each cell is uniquely loved and redeemed. The human race is not a haphazard aggregation, each entity bent on self-determination, but in gospel terminology a "flock." Only wolves and hireling shepherds are unwelcome into the fold . . . and this is because they have excluded themselves. □

INRI

THE SUFFERING OF JESUS

We are told in the *Fioretti* that "through love and compassion Francis was wholly changed into Jesus." This took place initially on Mount La Verna but persisted for the rest of the saint's life. The transformation seems to have been immediate, though clearly Francis had been preparing for it, without knowing what was to come, since he first set himself on the way to perfection. This kind of change is something which, less dramatically, should be taking place in all of us. The passage quoted adds: "The marks of the nails began anon to appear on the hands and feet of St. Francis." The word "anon" and later the words "after a space" would seem to show that the significant grace was the interior one of union and that the stigmata expressed it outwardly. For us who have not experienced the grace of transforming union a comparable process may be traced: a heightened awareness of Christ's love and of his Passion expressed outwardly in works of charity and acceptance of suffering.

Christ suffering extends himself in our sufferings: we suffer and so extend the merit of his suffering. St. Paul explains this to the Corinthians when he says: "We carry about continually in our bodies the dying state of Jesus so that the living power of Jesus may be manifested in our bodies too." Without the sufferings of Christ, in which our own sufferings find their place, there would be no merit in suffering. Suffering in itself is not a good but the denial of a good: for a Christian the whole value of suffering lies in its identification with Christ's Passion.

In the playing down of traditional devotions, particularly those which have to do with the sacred Passion, the faithful are losing their sense of oneness with the Crucified. We need to be reminded that we are members of a Body whose head is crowned with thorns, whose heart is open and bleeding, whose hands and feet are pierced with nails. Physical pain could be called a sacramental mystery whereby we are united with him who instituted the sacraments of which he is the fulfillment and the mysteries of which he is the author. Our Lord, raising pain from the physical to the spiritual, wants none of it to be wasted. Naturally we shrink from pain, as in his human nature he did too, but supernaturally we sanctify it by directing it towards his pain. The world aims at eliminating pain, or at least anaesthetizing it, while the Spirit invites us to make the most of it. The attitude of the saints toward suffering will be considered in another place, so all that need be said here is that pain was for them a veil through which they could see the sufferings of Christ. This did not lessen its hurt but it made pain into a prayer.

The story that the soldier who thrust a spear into our Lord's side was cured of a disease of the eyes by the blood and water which flowed from the wound may not have historical backing, but it certainly has a spiritual meaning for us. The soldier was not completely blind or he could not have seen the body to pierce it (let alone held his post in the army). Nor are we completely blind when confronted with the crucified Christ: we see the blurred figure, the hazy outline of the cross. Like breaking the legs of the prisoners, Longinus's act was in the line of duty. Our reaction to the Passion, at first anyway, is dutiful rather than from the heart, a routine piety rather than an outpouring of compassion. The mixture of water and blood washes the man's eyes and he sees. Water symbolizes cleansing; blood symbolizes life. When grace has come from Christ's body to ours, washing us in baptism and giving us life in the Eucharist, we see. The image of the Passion is now more than an image, more than a symbol. It is an experience which we, with our own sufferings, can share. We have no cause to envy Longinus his luminous vision—far more penetrating than the original gift of sight. □

THE DYING OF JESUS

The Roman soldiers watched our Lord die but gave him little attention; they were rolling dice at the time. Zacharias, five hundred years earlier, had prophesied that "they shall look on him whom they pierced." Mary, John and the holy women "looked on" the dead Christ but they had not pierced him. Nor had Nicodemus and Joseph. The crowds had gone, and the priests and Roman officials who were responsible for the piercing had not been present anyway. So apart from the unimpressed guards, who would not have stayed on longer than they had to, to whom is the prophesy most applicable? To ourselves. We are not in the position of casual bystanders or military torturers: we *know* that here is the Second Person of the Holy Trinity hanging dead on the cross. He has died for us; collectively but individually too. So if we have pierced him and are looking on, we must make sure that we see in right perspective. This we do best by "dying daily" with St. Paul; "Both in life and in death," says St. Paul again, "we are the Lord's."

While St. Paul is the chief exponent of dying to sin and living to Christ, St. John provides us with the most appropriate text for this section of the book when he says in Revelation: "Blessed are the dead who die in the Lord." Once again it refers to a sharing in all that Christ has to bring. Though the words may refer here to every soul who dies in a state of grace, they refer particularly to the soul that "lives in the Lord" by making him the goal of all desire. If we are seriously trying to live in the Lord, there is every reason to believe that we shall die in the Lord. Certainly to die outside the Lord would be the crowning tragedy for those who have lived without regard for him.

"Without Jesus Christ," wrote Pascal on the death of his father, "death is horrible. *In* Jesus Christ it is quite otherwise: it is something to be loved, it is holy, it is the joy of the faithful. Everything is sweet in Jesus Christ, even death, and this is why he has suffered and died—to sanctify suffering and death." In our consideration of death we make the mistake of thinking of it in isolation: either apart from Christ's death, as suggested in the Pascal quotation, or apart from heaven. The thought of death on its own is a negative thought. Without having consciously to trace the developing process, the more we think of Christ living within us, the more we think of his dying for us, and the more we think of Christ dying for us, the more we think of death—his and ours—in terms of the resurrection and heaven. No one knew this better than St. Paul. To the Romans: "Both in life and in death we are the Lord's . . . that is why Christ died and came to life again." To the Corinthians: "He died for all so that those who live might live no longer for themselves but for him who for their sakes died and was raised up." To the Philippians: "To me life means Christ; hence dying is so much gain . . . whether I live or die, Christ will be exalted through me." Life, death, heaven: to be thought of less as separate entities than as different aspects of the one entity, namely Christ.

Even had we no spiritual aspirations to act as incentive, psychologically we cannot help longing for something better than what we are getting here on earth. It is the work of grace so to train our desires on the absolute that we get our perspectives right. We see heaven as perfect and unending love, and everything else in relation to that. □

THE PERFECTION OF MARY

"Every living organism," according to St. Thomas, "strains towards its own proper perfection." If this is true, then from the toadstool to the orchid, from the tadpole to the buffalo, from the unthinking baby in the womb to the cleverest person on the earth, there is a designed growth of its own particular kind. The growth may be halted, may be diverted into channels which were not intended for it, but the appropriate goal for the appropriate species is there. Apart from her divine son, Mary is the only "organism" in the whole history of mankind who has attained to her "own proper perfection." This brings home to us the harm that original sin has done in the created order of being.

Theologians have debated whether Mary's perfection is different in kind or in degree from the perfection held out to us. The question is surely not how different it may be to ours but how like it *can* be to ours. There are two practical questions here: how far, by imitating her virtues, we can follow the path which she did, and how far we may presume to make her perfection ours. The first looks to our practice of humility, charity, detachment, dependence on God, and the second to our confidence in the efficacy of her merits in relation to ourselves.

Seeing into the mystery of the incarnation more deeply than anyone else, Mary could not but be more humble than anyone else. That she, a human being, was chosen by the Father to bring the Second Person the the Holy Trinity into the world made her aware, in a way which nothing else could have done, both of her own nothingness and of the power and goodness of God. The *Magnificat* exactly expresses this. From the womb of humility came forth the source and fulfillment of humility. In the same way Mary's charity must have been stronger than anyone else's who has ever lived because Mary was closer than anyone else to the personification of love, to love itself. This charity did not die when Mary ceased to live on earth—any more than the charity of Jesus died when his supreme act of charity was consummated on the cross—but lives in heaven where it finds even more perfect fulfillment than it found on earth. The virtues of detachment and dependence on God inevitably follow from humility and charity, and it will be by the help of Mary that we develop these her characteristic qualities. That Mary was obedient, patient, compassionate, prayerful—possessed of every virtue you can think of—was because her response to grace never faltered and knew no limit. In our degree, and handicapped as we are by original sin, we can nevertheless aspire, as she did while on earth, to perfect holiness. The means at hand are the same for us as they were for her. We too, if we try, can be humble, kind, detached, trusting in God and avoiding occasions of sin. Our perfection is now a matter of responding more and more to the action of grace. As the soul develops in spirituality the opportunities of grace are increasingly seen. At the Annunciation what did Mary know of the sorrows which were to be hers? The point is she was open to everything that grace should bring. Her readiness did not spring from her knowledge; her knowledge emerged gradually from her readiness. So long as we are ready to cooperate, to be generous, we can forget about the kind of perfection, the degree of perfection, that will be ours. □

THE MERITS OF MARY

While the recognition of Mary's place in our lives is primarily reflected in the attempt we make to follow her in the practice of her virtues, it is not only as an example that she is the object of our devotion. As an incentive to her service and to the service to the Father, she provides us with an inexhaustible fund of merit which we can draw upon in default of merit of our own. Mary's sinlessness goes bail for us who are loaded with guilt and liable for punishment either in this life or in purgatory. She is our advocate with the accumulated substance of her virtue to back her advocacy. She substitutes what she is and has for what we are not and for what we lack. One likes to think of Mary's hand coming down in the nick of time to alter the just sentence passed upon us to something milder, and in the case of the holy souls, to whisk them out of purgatory before their time. Reparation for sin is efficacious, mercifully, under her direction; it is woefully inadequate under ours.

Since Christ is the redeemer of mankind, and since Mary was one with him in all that he did on earth, and is one with him now in heaven, there should be no difficulty in believing that Mary fully cooperated with her son at the time of the crucifixion and cooperates with him now in extending the salvific grace to man. If we attain salvation not by any merit of ours but by Christ's merits, then in virtue of Mary's union with Jesus we inherit the benefits which come to us from mother as well as son. Those who feel uneasy about some of the titles given to Mary, and who hope that the doctrines of Co-redemptrix and Mediatrix will never become articles of faith, would find it helpful to approach the subject from the standpoint of Christ's mind rather than to reason their way towards a formula. It is the job of the teaching Church to frame formulae; it is the job of the praying Church to accept what help it can from traditional beliefs. Such help is given by Mary in her twofold activity of atoning and mediating.

The theory has been advanced that Mary's virtue, and therefore her merit, is greater than that of all the saints put together. While I personally am more than ready to believe this, there are two points I would like to see clarified. First, who said so? If the view represents the official teaching on Marian prerogatives, and has been held traditionally by the faithful, there is no problem. Secondly, how does the claim help? Faced with such a proposition we see immediately a pair of scales which has the virtues of millions piled up on one tray and the virtues of Mary on another—Mary's tray weighing heavier. Such a concept may increase the homage we give to our Lady—and if it does we should dwell upon it—but there is a danger that we place her on an altogether different plane from our own. The whole point is that she was, and is, one of us. "Blessed art thou *among* women," not remote from humankind but like in all things but sin. When we start balancing her merits and virtues against those of our fellow Christians we become like scientists comparing the atmosphere of outer space to our own. Though free of original and actual sin, Mary was very much of our planet.

It is anyway impossible for us to measure merit, so the sensible course to take is to ask our Lady to distribute its blessings to the souls who need them most. □

THE PRAYERS OF MARY

We know nothing of what prayers our Lady said or what heights her contemplation scaled. As regards vocal prayer it can be assumed that she recited the psalms and readings prescribed for Jewish families. She and St. Joseph would have been required to teach the rituals of liturgical worship to Jesus as a child. As to her interior prayer we can again only guess, for all we have to go on is the statement in St. Luke after he has described the finding in the Temple that "she pondered all these words in her heart." The only certain conclusion is that since Mary's life was perfect, her prayer was perfect too. Not that she was spared the necessity of working at the perfecting of her prayer, any more than she was spared the necessity of perfecting her virtue, but that at every stage her cooperation was perfect. There were distractions to be overcome—just as

Jesus was to overcome the distraction of fear in the Garden of Gethsemane, and the "distractions" of loneliness and despair on Calvary—but these served only to reinforce the application.

If no extraordinary phenomena—stigmata, levitations, bilocations and so on—are recorded as having a place in Mary's prayer, it means that either she did not experience them or that, if she did, it is not necessary for us to know about them. Either way we can conclude that such mystical manifestations are not to be equated with even perfect prayer, and that where they are found to occur they come as outward evidence of prayer and not as an essential quality or invariable consequence of pure prayer. This should dispose of the idea that it was Mary's prayer that "produced" the Angel Gabriel at the Annunciation. If Mary's prayer were to bring about no miracles, today or at any other time, it would still be perfect prayer. What is it that "magnifies the Lord"? "My soul" it is that gives glory to the Lord. My inward disposition is my prayer, even before it comes out in formulated acts. "All the glory of the King's daughter," says the psalmist, "is within." While this text should apply to every soul, it applies particularly to Mary.

Lacking precise information about her prayer we do better to speak of her devotion. *Vas devotionis;* the vessel is big enough to include prayer. But the term "devotion" must be rightly understood. Modern spiritual writers have shown that warm feelings do not constitute devotion, and that true devotion is in the will rather than in the emotions. It is alertness in the recognition of God's will and in the response to it. Mary's devotion was not a sudden uprush of fervor but a constant unfolding of herself in waiting upon the breath of the Spirit. Her devotion, containing her prayer, was inevitably a drawn-out offering. "To you, O Lord, do I lift up my soul"—now and at all times. The prayer act comprises surrender, trust, gratitude, longing, acceptance, self-forgetting: all compounded in the one actuation of love.

What can we learn from all this? Surely that Mary's "Be it done unto me according to thy word" can characterize our reaction to every happening of the day. In this way the inward, the essential prayer force, "informs" the outward. The outward, in the alchemy of grace, becomes prayer. It would be a mistake to imagine that fidelity to prayer began and ended with either printed prayers or fixed periods regulated by the clock. If our prayer is to be like Mary's, it must be an extended exercise. □

THE SUFFERINGS OF MARY

Suffering can be considered either as punishing or as purifying. In Jesus and Mary there was nothing which needed to be punished and nothing which admitted of purification. So the sufferings of Jesus and Mary come as a free gift to man: nothing has to be subtracted to cover debts of their own. Yet we know that Jesus and Mary suffered more than any other human beings that have ever lived. Just as we are made free of Christ's Passion, so we are made free of Mary's sorrows. If suffering is to be no more than endurance for endurance sake—something to be got through because it cannot be got out of—it may satisfy the requirement of punishment but of purification it will fall dismally short. It may even, when accompanied by resentment, bitterness, envy and self-pity, work away from purification. Mary's acceptance of suffering exactly reproduced her son's attitude towards it. Nothing supine or negative here, but on the contrary a will to sacrifice actively and positively. The point has been made that Mary *stood* at the foot of the cross, nearer to the heart of the Passion than sitting in the shadow of the cross.

The nearer *anyone* comes to the Passion the nearer that soul comes to sympathy and understanding. Mary was no exception here: suffering with Christ and with people, for Christ and for people. As mother of the crucified Jesus she is mother of compassion for human suffering. There can be no suffering that Mary does not know all about, and this is worth remembering when we have to endure the suffering of temptation. Where questions of fear, doubt, frustrated hope and physical pain are concerned we may be ready enough to turn to Mary for help, but when it comes to attacks upon our lower nature, we tend to think that our Lady must be so far above all that sort of thing that it would be indelicate to invoke her help at such a level. Yet if Jesus "became sin" for the sake of sinful man, Mary must have joined her son in this as in everything else. Jesus, in taking on our human nature, did not take on only our higher nature but the whole of it; Mary, in compassionating the trials of our human nature, compassionates us in all our trials and at every level.

Jesus puts his undeserved sufferings at our disposal and Mary does the same. Punishment and purification are alike vicarious. Man, with the Magi at the Epiphany, may bring gifts to the Savior of the world, but Jesus and Mary do better than that: they bring themselves and their suffering to the work of saving the world. On an earlier page we have used the simile of scales to illustrate a comparison. This time we can instance an actual mural in a pre-Reformation English church. Mary is shown standing back from the two balances and dropping the beads of her rosary into one of them. The other tray or bowl is piled high with a great crowd of sinners. The few beads on the one side vastly outweigh the volume of the other which, to everyone's relief, soars into the sky.

"Whatever excellence a man possesses," says St. Thomas, "is given to him for the common good." Rightly understood, suffering is an excellence. At one time or another it is an excellence possessed by all of us. We should not be content to use it only for God. If we use it rightly for God, we use it in compassion for the good of others. The danger is that we do not use it at all. This is the real waste—that it should be punishment without purification. □

THE WORK OF MARY

Whatever the vocation, there is no compulsion. A particular work, even a particular kind of life, is offered to us. Whatever the determinists say, we are free to take it or leave it. But having accepted it, we can make the work or way of life pleasing to God and fruitful for ourselves only by yielding to it—by making it our own and God's. You might say that Mary's chance of working for God was offered to her when the Lord's angel declared the Father's message. But long before that she had chosen to spend her life for God. She had followed her attraction, the attraction of grace, and though she may have planned for herself a special form of service—as revelations to certain souls would claim—she yet remained open to whatever was in store.

To be the mother of the Messias, who was at the same time God, must of course be thought of as

Mary's principal work. Grace had prepared her for this vocation so that when it was made known to her she followed it. "Be it done unto me according to thy word": before and after the Annunciation, before and after Calvary. The incarnation, with its logical fulfilment in the atonement and resurrection, must inevitably have drawn the whole of Mary's spirituality into a single direction and into unity. But this does not mean it left man's needs out of account. Quite the reverse. We benefit all the more, not all the less, from Mary's singleminded dedication to divine love. "Behold your son . . . behold your mother." In committing John to his mother's care, Jesus, in the traditional interpretation, extends Mary's role of motherhood so that it embraces all mankind. If she had a personal responsibility before, she has a universal one now. With Christ we are part of her family, and she has the authority to counsel, correct, intercede, crown. If you want to know how concerned she is about sinners, holy souls in purgatory, the faithful, the ignorant and the dying, you have only to study what she said when appearing at Lourdes, Fatima and elsewhere.

If Mary did not possess the powers which we attribute to her, what would be the point of calling upon her for help? To be beautiful, sinless, queenly, enjoying a unique place in heaven would not help if we could not count upon her influence both in the Church and in our own affairs. "Pray for us sinners now and at the hour of our death." This goes beyond acknowledgment; it is an appeal. When Mordecai put it to his niece Esther, "Who knows but it was for a time like this that you obtained the royal dignity?" he was unconsciously hailing Mary, who was not to be born for nearly four hundred years. And in Jeremias there is the prophetic text pointing to Mary in her role of advocate: "Remember that I have stood in thy sight to speak good for them and to turn thine indignation from them." These are not the pleadings of a slave, but reminders of a prerogative, a prerogative of mercy.

If she carried weight in our Lord's lifetime, as we know from the Cana incident that she did, she does so still. Where Jesus honored her wishes when he was a child at Nazareth, he honors her wishes now that he is at the right hand of the Father. Each time she reveals herself to souls today, and never have her appearances been more frequent, she promises, on evidence of our penitence, to obtain a reprieve of the sentence which our sins have earned. □

THE CROWNING OF MARY

In giving to Mary the title Queen of Heaven we must steer clear of the Cinderella syndrome—the humble maiden raised to a rank undreamed of by her sisters. Since Mary was unique in the privilege of her birth, it is a necessary consequence that her place in heaven is uniquely privileged too. Closer than anyone else to her son on earth, she remains closer than anyone else to her son in heaven. We think of the crown, the sceptre, the royal robe, but these are only the symbols; more significant is the place which she occupies in the divine mind and the authority that is vested in her. The idea "sovereign lady" fires the imagination. We think of subjects bowing down in homage, the coronation ceremony with its silver trumpets and display of gold plate, rich materials, thrones and jewels. In other words we picture a monarch such as we have seen in technicolor films, and then project the image, limitlessly enhanced, until it represents the ideal queen. What we forget is that divine royalty came first, and whatever queenliness a human representative can show is only a blurred likeness held up to the prototype. Earthly kings and queens are derivations only, owing their title and estate to the originals. Christ the king of kings, Mary the queen of queens: what temporal ruler can be sure of such a decent place in history when the crowned in heaven command praise and devotion for all eternity?

In the Litany of Loreto, and in other prayers, Mary is named as queen of this and that; and the fifth glorious mystery of the rosary commemorates her crowning in heaven. Honor given to Mary, under whatever title, is always a sign of health. But again there is room for misplaced devotion. Mary may not be thought of in the way that pagan cults think of a goddess. We pay homage to her as the patron of virtues, occupations, places, churches and shrines, but not as deity. Mary's nobility is borrowed from the absolute nobility of God. "He who is powerful has done great things in me: I am his handmaid." It is right that we should acknowledge Mary as queen over many aspects of our life, over every activity of the Church's life, but all this is summed up when we call her Queen of Love.

Romanesque carving in stone, gothic carving in stone and wood, baroque carving gilded and glittering: the crowning of Mary has been the subject of art for centuries, and religous art, like religious literature and music, reflects at any period the mind of the faithful. Not so well known as most of his other paintings, Fra Angelico's rendering of the coronation of Mary and the saints does more than canonize in color a traditional theme: it is the crowning of joy. Mary, the saints, the angels, the clouds, the grass and sky—they ring out joy like a peal of bells. Perhaps this is one reason why the coronation has been so widely commemorated. However black the Church's dark periods and however depressed the spirit of the world, joy has a way of breaking through. Jesus came bringing joy, a joy which Mary has radiated ever since. *Causa nostrae laetitiae . . . Mater jucunditatis . . . ora pro nobis.* □

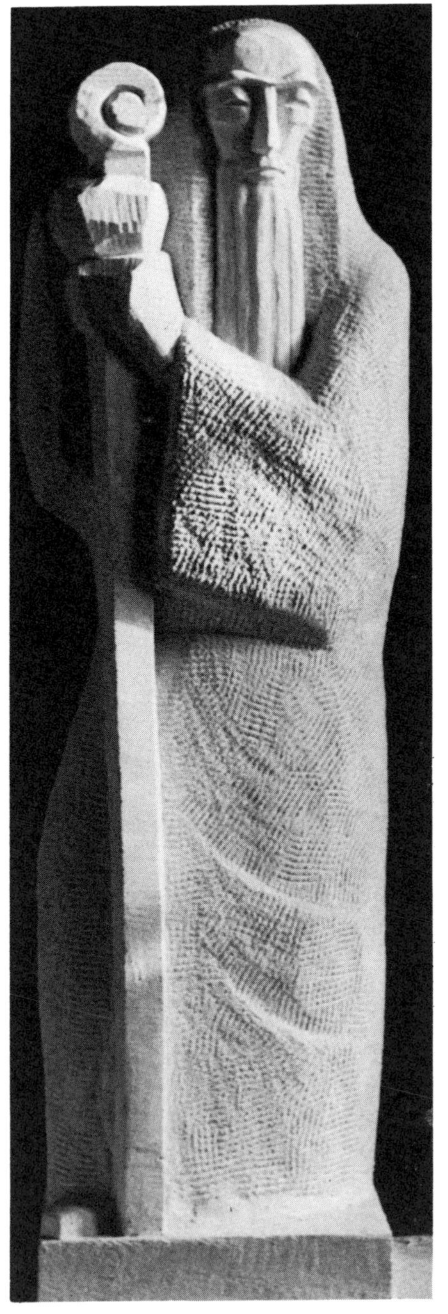

THE ROLE OF THE SAINTS

The whole point of holiness, the first purpose, is to give glory to God. People do not become saints to better themselves. The process is this: God gives his love to souls, and the degree to which souls return his love is the measure of their sanctity. It is not as if God puts in a peg and says, "Beyond this peg you are a saint; short of it you are not." What he says is "Keep on trying to love and leave the measuring to me." So since it is a matter of interior relationship to God, the "role" of the saints is not always something which can be seen. The secondary role of the saints is to leaven the lump of fallen humanity. The form taken by this leavening process—which will vary with each saint, with the particular need of his apostolate, with the direction of his particular grace and appropriate vocation, even with the period and country in which God has placed him—is determined only insofar as it is the most propitious setting for the exercise of love.

Sanctity is a consummation, a crowning gift from God, and not a self-imposed discipline. Nor is it a matter of temperament, a pious disposition leading on from unworldliness to the cultivation of the natural virtues. We tend to think of sanctity as a personal achievement and not as a free gift. The principle is stated in two of the Prefaces in the Missal: "It is only by your gift to us that we can give you thanks and prepare ourselves for salvation . . . in crowning the merits of the saints you crown your own gifts." The influence of the saints upon the world is the redirecting of what God has given to them. God is distributing his own gifts and using people to deliver them.

Even the hidden sanctity of those whose names never come up for beatification works as a leaven, and no less powerfully by being secret. The enclosed religious may exercise an apostolate as fruitfully as a saintly public figure. God raised up St. Teresa of Lisieux in order to stress this truth. The term "raised up" is perhaps unfortunate in this connection, suggesting that the soul had no say in the matter. The idea of being dragooned into sanctity would be false. There is a difference in being compelled by force and impelled by the movement of grace. Souls are drawn by the Holy Spirit—*caritas Christi urget nos*—or they would never get started, but they are never so pressurized as not to be free. They may not operate their own sanctity, but they must cooperate in it. So when we speak of saints being raised up to counter a particular evil or to preach a particular doctrine we mean that God in his eternal providence foresees a situation which calls for heroic virtue. He sends someone who is a potential saint to do the work. The person remains potential while God gives him graces appropriate to the job. The potential may or may not be realized, but where it is you have the saint.

In spite of what people say, nobody fulfills himself. All a man can do is to present himself as an empty vessel before God and ask to be filled by grace to the level desired by God. There is much spiritual wisdom in Cardinal Merry del Val's prayer "that others become holier than I, provided that I may become as holy as I should." □

THE DIVERSITY OF THE SAINTS

"Each one reaches heaven," says Le Cardonel, "by climbing his own particular stairway." No two stairs are alike, but all agree on the way: the way is Christ. The simile can be developed endlessly. Not every soul, for example, reaches the same floor; some have to go down to the basement and begin again; handrails are provided for those who need them but there is no getting off to use a lift; the lights may go out; the carpet may slip; other climbers may overtake you, bump into you, laugh at you, trip you up. The mistake is to delay too long on one step when you should be moving. Better to arrive out of breath than to halt and give up.

When St. Augustine discourses at length on "the two lives," he may be felt to overlook the many lives which lie in between. "One is the life of faith," he says, "the other the life of knowledge;

one the life of work, the other the life of rest; one the life of action, the other the life of contemplation." He qualified this black-and-white distinction in another treatise where he says, "God works in a most manifold way, being all things in each single thing and one in all of them together." This is surely much more like it: not two lives but as many as there are souls to live them, not two ways but as many as there are souls to move along them.

It is a question of individual vocation. The only obstacle to finding God's vocation for *me* is my own self-will. Provided I look for God's will, and do not delude myself into thinking my will is his, there is nothing in the world to prevent me from finding it—and ultimately from finding sanctity. Sins do not get in the way of sanctity nearly so much as modelling oneself upon a particular interpretation of sanctity and following a particular regimen of sanctity. "Men wise in their own conceits," says Tauler, "will bid you do this and do that to become perfect, and it will be all a set of observances of their own contrivance." The true saint will not only avoid the doctrinaire in his own spiritual life but will be careful not to impose a routine on other people. This accounts for the variety which is to be found among God's saints. Each one builds on his God-given temperament with the particular grace of his vocation. It is no good modelling myself on the father of the desert if God has called me to be a taxi-driver.

So it is not simply to provide us with patrons who will help us in our differing careers that God gives us such a wide range of saints. Much more it is to encourage us to believe that no career, unless it is opposed to religion, excludes the possibility of sanctity. With so many unlikely people becoming saints, we take heart and feel drawn to make the effort. God could have standardized sanctity but instead diversified it. Just as in nature he could have decreed that there should be one kind of tree, one kind of climate, one kind of illness (what would we have had to talk about if our insides were all the same?) so in the approach to holiness the souls are not restricted to parallel lines. It is a question of direction, not regimentation; of love and not distance covered. "In my Father's house there are many mansions," each one filled with love. □

S· FIACRE

THE UNITY OF THE SAINTS

From what has been said in the foregoing section it follows that out of the many understandings of love some sort of consistent pattern must emerge or there will be no proof that love forms a unifying link. The gospel supplies this pattern. "If any man will be my disciple let him deny himself, take up his cross, and follow me." Primary condition: self-surrender. "I do always the will of my heavenly Father": the way we show we are disciples. "He who hears you, hears me; and he who hears me hears also my Father who is in heaven": obedience to divinely constituted authority. "Man does not live by bread alone but by every word that proceeds from the Father": belief in scripture. "If you do not love your brother whom you see, how can you love God whom you do not see?": charity. "Judge not and you shall not be judged . . . forgive and you shall be forgiven":

bearing no grudge. And the basic condition of all: "If you love me keep my commandments." Love expressed in faith and faith expressed in love. "Without faith you cannot do anything," but when we examine the nature of this faith we find it amounting to the soul's response to love, and therefore it is itself love.

Other marks of sanctity there are—joy, peace, zeal for souls, reverence for the church—but these come rather as a consequence of sanctity than as partaking of its essence. Thus you can expect a saint to possess discernment of spirits, but this will be accidental and not necessarily invariable. You would like your saint to be raised in ecstasy when he prays, but again this does not have to be. It would be convenient if every saint were to cure the sick and raise the dead, but not all saints are called to do these things. These are works performed in virtue of the inward activity of love, and the inward activity reveals itself in different ways. In his letter to the Corinthians St. Paul makes the point clear:

"There are different works but the same God who accomplishes all of them . . . to one the Spirit gives wisdom in discourse, to another the power to express knowledge . . . by the same Spirit another is given the gift of healing, and still another miraculous powers . . . but it is one and the same Spirit who produces all these gifts, distributing to each as he wills."

St. Paul then goes on to give the analogy of the body with its many members—"whether Jew or Greek, slave or free." The passage concludes with the words "Now I will show you the way which surpasses all the others," and his thirteenth chapter is the description, the summing up in fact, of love.

So if we are looking for the "bond of perfection" we get it in as many words from St. Paul. "No other foundation is laid but that which is laid, which is Christ Jesus," and on that foundation we are being "built up into this temple to become a dwelling place for God in the Spirit." Where the bond is charity, the bond is Christ. Where the foundation is Christ, the foundation is charity.

Since "God rewards only his own works," the soul who wants to be holy must make sure that what is worked is worked in charity and not in self-will. On the impulse of self great works may, outwardly, be achieved. On the impulse of charity the achievement, outwardly, may be negligible. Which is more important, love or results? *Caritas Christi urget nos.* The results can look after themselves. □

THE EXPERIENCE OF THE SAINTS

After saying how varied are the vocations of the saints, it would be rash to generalize about their experience. If one common feature stands out, however, it is that they were frustrated in their desires—even in their most selfless aspirations—and that far from being defeated they overcame the drawbacks, psychological as well as material, which they met with on their way to God. It is the story of the burning bush in Moses' vision: always threatened with extinction but never consumed. This is only what might be expected when the model of all saints experienced failure, rejection, suffering, death, and then rose again in triumph.

We get it all in St. Paul. To the Corinthians he writes: "We are afflicted in every way possible but are not crushed; full of doubts we never despair. We are persecuted but never abandoned; we are struck down but never destroyed." He goes on to give the secret of this renewal: "Continually we carry in our bodies the dying of Jesus . . . while we live we are constantly being delivered to death for Jesus' sake so that the life of Jesus may be revealed in our mortal flesh." St. Paul might almost be commenting on the burning bush revelation when he says "our inner being is renewed each day though our body is being destroyed at the same time." The source of our revivication is, as we have seen throughout this book, the hidden activity of Christ within the soul. It is, moreover, an activity revived daily, hourly, all the time, and not something which we decide to refurbish every now and then as in times of retreat or at particular seasons of the liturgy.

If St. Paul's writings outline the pattern of sanctity, his own experience, inward and outward, may be taken as typical. Interiorly he was unable to escape the temptation which he calls the sting of his flesh; exteriorly he came up against every obstacle to his apostolate. Having suffered beatings, stonings, three shipwrecks and betrayals from his brethren, he met with what must have seemed the death blow to his mission when he was imprisoned in Rome. Yet in fact it was from prison that he launched the most effective of his missions. It was as if in his cell he was handed a microphone which was to speak to the whole world. He tells the Philippians about this:

"I want you to know that my situation has worked out to the furtherance of the gospel. My imprisonment in Christ's cause has become well known throughout the praetorium here and to others as well. Most of my brothers in Christ, taking courage from my chains, have been further emboldened to speak the word of God fearlessly."

His experience of frustration has fired the enthusiasm of others, and so the gospel spreads.

The moral of all this is surely that when thwarted either in the spiritual or active life we must believe that God will raise a phoenix from the ashes and that blackening cinders are the most effective kind of kindling. When opportunities are cut off and circumstances are against us, then is the time to trust. When at our weakest then are we strong. Look at St. Ignatius, St. Teresa and St. John of the Cross, St. Benedict Joseph Labre, Mary Ward, Padre Pio: all had to endure the cross of failure and the crushing of their hopes. In the Preface for saints we have: "You have given us their way of life as a model." Meeting with apparently insuperable opposition in trying to follow Christ, we are in fellowship with the martyrs who experienced the ultimate frustration in this life as a prelude to eternal victory in the next. In the blackest moments of his life the saint clings to the word *virescit* and adds *in Christo.* □

THE GLORY OF THE SAINTS

The saints were the last people in the world to look for glory during their lifetime, so when they find posterity bestowing it upon them when they are dead they are not likely to notice the accolade. With the angels, the saints in heaven are occupied in loving, giving praise, and standing before God's throne in awe and wonder. The work of interceding for souls on earth and in purgatory is part of the glory they give to God, part of their love. They are only doing what Mary is doing—namely, drawing upon the infinite merits of Jesus. All personal glory, theirs and Mary's alike, comes from God and goes back to God. The saints in heaven understand now, in a way that they could not have understood fully while on earth, that every good is a borrowed good and that there is nothing that anyone can call his own. "Name something that you have not received," St.

Paul challenges the Corinthians, "and if you have received it why are you boasting as if it were yours?" Whatever glory there may be is the imputed glory of God.

If this is so and the saints have no glory of their own, it might be asked, why have a devotion to them? The answer is that from their place in heaven, enjoying the beatific vision, they pass on the prayers which come haltingly from us on earth. To have patrons in heaven is not something to be despised. We need all the help we can get.

But as a doctrine, the communion of saints means more than having a claim on someone in heaven who happens to bear the same name as you do. It means that all who are "reconciled in one body through Christ's cross" can comfort themselves with the knowledge that they belong already to the company of the saints. "You are no longer strangers and aliens," St. Paul writes to the Ephesians, "but fellow citizens with the saints and members of the household of God." Though not of saintly quality, as the term is generally understood, we are counted as though we were. Nor is this just a holy fiction in the matter of a label. "When you were dead in your sins," St. Paul explains to the Colossians, "God gave you *new life* in Christ." Ours is a victory over the law of sin: we "triumph in the person of Christ." Accordingly St. Paul, not tied down to subsequent terminology, calls all Christians who have renounced sin by the title of "saint." Indeed we are called to *be* saints. "God has called us to a holy life, not because of any merit of ours," Timothy is reminded, "but according to his own design," and to the Ephesians again, "God chose us in him before the world began to be holy and blameless in his sight, to be full of love." Our Lord himself summons us to "be perfect as your heavenly Father is perfect."

To conclude, what in practical terms constitutes sanctity? Love in heart and in expression must obviously come first. This leads to doing for God what is ordinarily done for self. But doing is not the whole story because the dynamic is being what man was, before the fall, designed to be; then only does man act as he was empowered to act. For this the soul needs three things: trust, the vision brought about by faith and prayer, and willingness to begin again after every failure. Trust: that God's grace will effect what is demanded and that the appropriate environment has been providentially planned. Vision: seeing life, the world, suffering, the whole human condition as God sees it. Perseverance: the constant desire, if not always acting consistently with the desire, to continue in the search—the incidence of failure not to be taken as the final word. The first and final word is love. He who is love is the alpha and omega. He is the sum of all. □

AN APPRECIATION

When did you last look at a baby picture of yourself? It's been a while since I myself came across one of those which my mother treasures. But who can forget how those brownish photographs intrigue and tickle and abash us all at once. My mother used to have a knack for producing that old album at the most inopportune moments. She might, for instance, treat a new girlfriend of mine, whom I was ever so eager to impress, to front, back, and side views of the family's firstborn in his diapers. Then I had to face little me lying on a fur rug and trying to raise that bald head only a mother could love; little me smiling with a toothless mouth from ear to ear; little me posing in his birthday suit and grinning, with no self-consciousness at all, straight at self-conscious big me.

I could not help remembering the challenge of

that childhood album when I read Dom Hubert van Zeller's book *To Be In Christ.* It is a book that makes us Catholic Christians face our recent past—in whatever light we may regard it. Like snapshots in an album, his meditations show us who we are by showing us who we were.

I was a novice at Mount Savior Monastery when Dom Hubert preached at our annual retreat there more than a quarter of a century ago. Ever since, I have thought of that senior monk as one of my great teachers and have tried to live by the guidance he gave us. Only a few days ago I found myself quoting him again with gratefulness. In fact, I can hardly speak about prayer without quoting him. To this day I have kept the notes I scribbled down during that retreat long ago in a handwriting that is no longer mine. In reading *To Be In Christ,* I find much of what I used to admire then: here is a writer who knows how to make a point, how to be succinct and yet explicit, how to quote the Bible. His most captivating passages are ones in which you can hear him chuckling under his breath. But I found more than I expected, more than is written in these pages, even between the lines. An old photograph shows us more than a picture can hold. It makes us see the invisible. It makes us see time. This book makes us realize how much history of spirituality we've lived through lately.

Life in Christ is the topic of this book. And "Jesus Christ [is] the same yesterday, today, and forever." We have the word of the Bible as witness. Why, then, the feeling of historic distance many readers of these meditations may experience? The reason is language, I submit. But language is more than words. It is a framework for seeing the world. As we frame our ideas in order to express them, we cannot help excluding whatever will not fit into the chosen frame. The language we choose to express our vision limits that vision, even our vision of revealed truth. Jesus Christ remains the same yesterday, today, and forever, but our angle of vision changes.

My veneration for Dom Hubert van Zeller makes it easy for me to hear in his words the same truth which I myself would express in very different language today. If within my own lifetime ways of speaking about our faith have had to change rather drastically in order to keep up with new insights, how much more in the long centuries of Christian tradition? A new angle of vision calls for new expression. But the truth (always seen only in part and only in part expressed) remains the same truth.

I am grateful that *To Be In Christ* confronts me both with the truth and with this truth about the truth. The change of outlook among Christians since the time when van Zeller first wrote (and helped bring about that change by his own writings) is more drastic than all the changes of the preceding thousand years together. Where it is love that speaks and love that listens, the changes do matter, but the unchanging truth matters more. Love is one, yet love speaks many languages.

Love rejoices in variety. To quote our author, "God could have standardized sanctity but instead diversified it. 'In my Father's house there are many mansions,' each one filled with love . . . Sins do not get in the way of sanctity nearly so much as modelling oneself upon a particular interpretation of sanctity . . . The true saint will not only avoid the doctrinaire in his own spiritual life but will be careful not to impose a routine on other people."

Why, then, should we insist on one language for speaking about life in Christ? To be in Christ means to be in the One who touches the extremes, who stretches out his strong and gentle arms and holds together beginning and end, what was and what will be, the old and the new. Dom Hubert van Zeller speaks of Him in a language that is certainly not the language of the eighties. But he speaks with love. If we listen with love, we shall find our true unchanging self—like a man who finds himself in the snapshot of a boy in a sailor suit. If we listen with love, we shall find the One who says, "Before Abraham was, I am." □

Brother David Steindl-Rast
Mt. Savior Monastery

APPENDIX

An artist-craftsman may not be the best judge of his work, but when making a selection with a view to publishing illustrations, he listens to nobody. This is only a way of saying that I have picked out the pieces which, over a period of fifty years, happen to please me most. It will be noticed that only stone carvings are here represented. This is partly because the works in wood and clay which I have undertaken are mostly scattered beyond recall and partly because those which I have been able to trace are not much good. Unless one is a Michelangelo or a Mestrovic, both of whom could handle different materials with equal confidence, a sculptor does well to choose his appropriate medium and stick to it. Barlach experimented in bronze and brass but came down firmly in favor of wood. Epstein tried stone but was far more successful with bronze. Noguchi, the contemporary Japanese sculptor, has worked with clay, wood, aluminum and steel, but has always come back to stone, which he calls "the basic element of sculpture, the unassailable absolute."

I would like to have included prints of a set of stations of the cross, carved in stone and now in a church in Pittsburgh, but since these have appeared in a book called *Approach to Calvary* and are also printed in paperback by the Downside Abbey Bookshop and Gallery, it seemed a mistake to overload the collection given here. Further plates have been used to illustrate *Approach to Christian Sculpture* (both issued by Sheed and Ward, and now out of print), so they have been discarded for the same reason. Photographs have appeared also in *Liturgical Art* and *Ars Sacra,* to the editors of which I am gratefully indebted.

In addition to the friends who have supplied me with photographs and whose names are listed below, I must express my especial thanks to two, namely to Mr. John Deline and Baron Nicolas van den Branden de Reeth, without whose help I could not have put this book together. Mr. Deline has gone to great trouble in having photographs copied and in investigating the possibilities of publication. Baron Nicolas van den Branden de Reeth has handed over his collections of photographs when all but a few of my own were stolen. To both these friends I am extremely grateful.

Acknowledged also with gratitude are the following who, whether alive or now dead, have taken the photographs: Dom Denis Agius, Mr. John Barlow, Dom Clement Birch, the late Dom Alban Brooks, Mr. Brian Cotton, the late Lord Craven, Miss Kathleen Eachus, Mr. Dmitri Kasterine, Mr. John Mosley, Mr. Douglas Steuert, Dom Stephen Tweedie, and Miss Jeanne Whitman. □

LIST OF PHOTOGRAPHS